Kindness   Perspective   Social Intelligence

Showing Compassion and Kindness
Dialling up Social Intelligence and Perspective

Written and Illustrated by Tenille Dowe
Copyright © 2024 Tenille Dowe (Images and Writing)

All rights reserved. No part of this book may be reproduced in any manner whatsoever without prior written permission of the publisher.

© Copyright 2004-2024, VIA Institute on Character. All Rights Reserved. Used with Permission.
www.viacharacter.org

First Printing, 2024

Published by Creative Heart Connection

www.creativeheartconnection.com
Creative Heart Connection
creative.heart.connection

ISBN 978-1-7636536-0-3

Showing Compassion and Kindness

Dialling up Social Intelligence and Perspective

Written and Illustrated
by Tenille Dowe

Sometimes we can feel sad.
This feels like there are dark clouds everywhere.

It can feel like there is no sunshine.

Kindness and compassion are
like sunshine on a rainy day.

This is like a warm hug.

Kindness and compassion are shown by lending an ear to listen.

Sharing a smile, or a kind gesture or asking 'Are you ok?"

Being socially intelligent means you are able to understand how others might feel. This is called empathy.

Empathy is the ability to emotionally understand what others feel, see things from their point of view and imagine yourself in their place.

Social intelligence is tuning in to the emotions, thoughts, and intentions of others in a positive way.

We respond in a way that demonstrates positive connections and compassion for others.

Together, they create a space where our friends feel seen and heard.

> We can put ourselves in the other person's shoes to understand how they might be feeling. This is called empathy.

Small acts of kindness ripple outwards, making the world a brighter, more compassionate place for all.

Imagine if someone doesn't understand how to be kind. It could be like being caught in the rain without an umbrella.

Social intelligence is being able to understand how others are feeling.

We are all friends, but that doesn't mean we all see things the same way.

We could have different perspectives and experiences and that is alright.

We all see the world through our own lens and experiences. This is called perspective.

I see an 'M', but my friend sees a 'W'.
What we see can depend on where we are standing or the experience we have.

The image we see is exactly the same.
However, some will see a vase.

While others see two side profiles of a face.

There is no right or wrong.
Just different perspectives.

This can be frustrating and lead to misunderstandings and conflict.

www.ingramcontent.com/pod-product-compliance
Lightning Source LLC
Chambersburg PA
CBRC091722070526
44585CB00007B/149